SEEK & FIND

Sp7t

7

By KIDSLABEL

School

chronicle books·san francisco

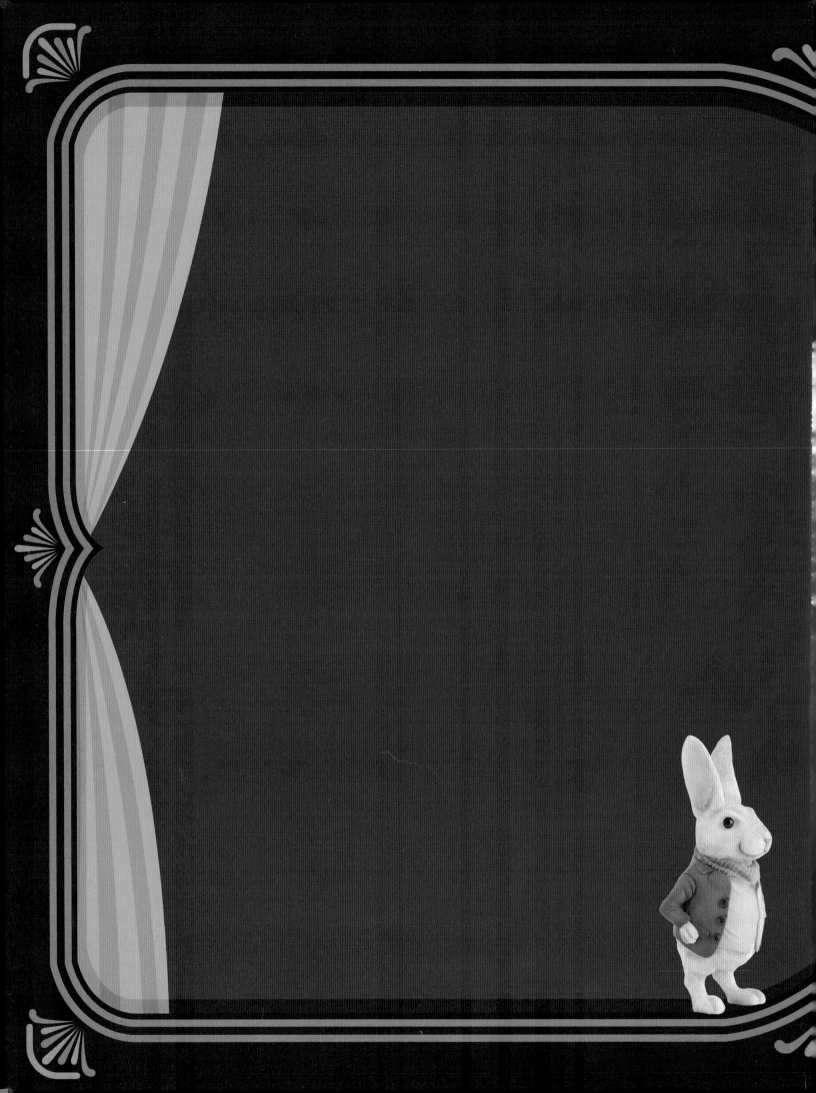

The pairs of photos in this book of picture riddles seem the same...

**but look carefully.
There are 7 differences.**

You'll also find a **riddle** below each pair of photos.
Need a **clue?** The answer is always something
in the picture above.

Extra Challenge
Looking only at the right-hand pages (and don't forget
the front cover!), find:

4 **aces**
6 **clocks**
10 **rabbits**
10 **shuttlecocks**
14 **paint tubes**
15 **robots**

and the white rabbit's pocket watch.

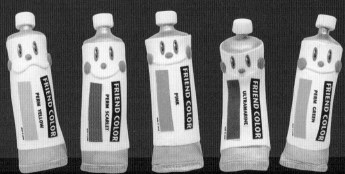

This glass is not for drinking.
Your reflection's not inside.
But look through it and you'll find
the smallest details cannot hide.

My first's in neither sun nor moon, but you can find it in the sky.
My second's in the desert, but stays away from dry.
My third is always part of you, but is never found in me.
My whole is known for making safe and also setting free.

Hint: This is a spelling riddle.

1._____ 2._____ 3._____

I have no mouth with which to speak it,
so if you ask, I cannot say.
And though I work so hard to keep it,
my face and hands give it away.

...What am I?

I'm a tough guy, hard-headed.
Give me a strong arm,
and I'll get the job done.
Just watch your fingers.

From my mouth a single note
Repeats. With my brothers I greet and
Orchestrate the twilight with a
Green and leaping song.

Strike me; you'll see
my anger's hot and quick.
But when I've cooled down,
I'm just a stick.

Pinch me and I'll hold the line.
I'll help things hang around
and neither give them to the wind
nor let them touch the ground.

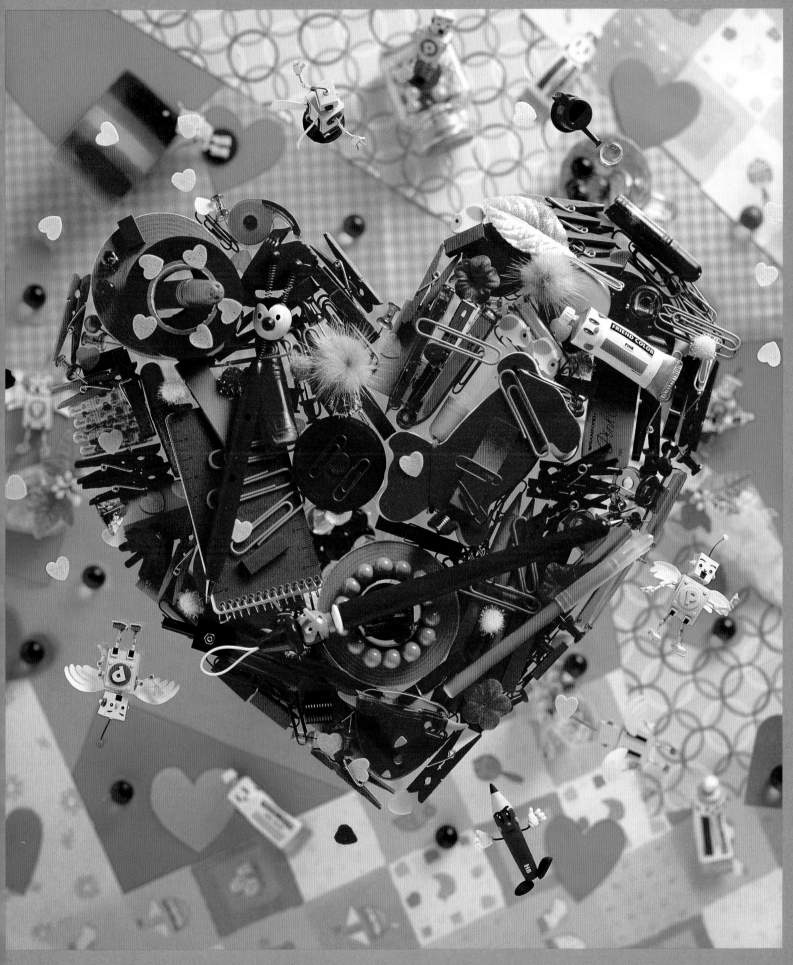

$3+2=5, 6+7=1, 1-4=\square$

I am not king or queen
or president.
But I am meant to rule.
What am I?

It has no wings, but it can fly.
It's fittest when it's fat.
But if it's lost its breath,
it's flat.

Sally wore a red dress
and lived up in a tree.
When she came down she gave up
her stony heart to me.

I'm with you running or resting,
at home, at school, in the park.
Where you go I must follow—
unless you go in the dark.

I'm certainly quite toothy
but I haven't any bite.
And if you have a knotty problem,
I'll quickly set it right.

Front and Back Covers: Look for

a pink dot on a yellow bug
a lion in a matchbox
a rocket's fire
a yellow bead by a red star
an orange jelly bean
a bead to the left of a green die
a clear yellow die

Backpack Treasures: Look for

a pebble with lines of red
a globe
some scissors
a magnifying glass
a blue bead by a green marble
a rocket ship
a blue marble by some blue rope

Let the Games Begin: Look for

a red spot by a tower of backgammon
   pieces
a rabbit by a pillow
an airplane
a dartboard
a globe
a purple block
a backgammon piece that's been
   turned over

In the Hall: Look for

a minute hand
a blackboard
a stripy bag
a red die
the queen of hearts
a rabbit
a red backpack

Arts and Crafts: Look for

a mallet
a heart by a banana
a spot of red by a pot of yellow
a paint tube by some pens
a hat on a clay dog
many paint tubes on a shelf
a hat on a bust

Music: Look for

a frog on a keyboard
a white dot on a guitar
a red marble on some orange ribbon
a key that's just a little lower
a trumpet valve
a pairs of castanets
a little guy on a maraca

Science: Look for

a stick of yellow chalk by a test tube
   of blue liquid
a piece of litmus paper in a matchbox
a thermometer
two microscope lenses
a drawing of a flask
a test tube that's a bit more full

School Supplies: Look for

a robot near the top
a heart by a pushpin by a pink pom-pom
a red paper clip on a red button
a red pom-pom on a red dog
a green marble on the left
a pink square on some pink tape
a clear bead by a watering can

In the Classroom: Look for

a plastic pencil box
a rabbit
a book in a desk
a pencil sharpener
a yellow chalkboard eraser
a blue question mark
a round green magnet

P.E.: Look for

a yellow ball
a number 1
the ace of hearts
a unicycle's pedal
some hula hoops
some red plastic chain
a number next to 5

Rock, Paper, Scissors: Look for

a hand
a thumb
a hand with a heart ring
a pink candy by a red gummi bear and
   a cow
a spot on a cow
a pink wafer by a rabbit's paw
a pair of yellow ducks

Recess!: Look for

a person's shadow
a rabbit's whiskers
a tennis ball by an in-line skate
a tennis ball by a tennis racquet
a baseball glove
an aluminum can
a painted rock

Favorite Things: Look for

something pink by a robot
a clear bead on an apple
a heart full of lipgloss
a bear's arm
something red between two different hearts
a tin with white hearts
the center of a flower

Answers to the riddles:

Backpack Treasures: magnifying glass
Let the Games Begin: key
In the Hall: clock
Arts and Crafts: mallet
Music: frog (this one's an acrostic: the first
   letter of each line spells the answer)
Science: match
School Supplies: clothespin
In the Classroom: ruler
P.E.: ball
Rock, Paper, Scissors: cherry
Recess!: shadow
Favorite Things: comb

Still can't find them?
Look at our Web page!

http://www.chroniclebooks.com/spot7

more!
Spot some ∧ fun in

available wherever books are sold.

I love feathers best when still attached;
I love to bathe, but dislike wet;
I like to play with my food.
I *hate* the vet.

First published in the United States in 2006 by Chronicle Books LLC.

Copyright © 2003 KIDSLABEL Corp.
English text © 2006 by Chronicle Books LLC.
First published in Japan in 2003 under the title
Doko Doko? Seven 3. Tomodachi by KIDSLABEL Corp.
English translation rights arranged with KIDSLABEL Corp.
through Japan Foreign-Rights Centre.

English type design by Brenden Mendoza.
Typeset in Super Grotesk.
Manufactured in China.

Library of Congress Cataloging-in-Publication Data
KIDSLABEL.
  Spot 7 School / by KIDSLABEL.
     p. cm.
  ISBN-13: 978-0-8118-5324-8
  ISBN-10: 0-8118-5324-1
  1. Picture puzzles—Juvenile literature. I. Title.
  GV1507.P47F85 2006
  793.73—dc22
  2005026114

Distributed in Canada by Raincoast Books
9050 Shaughnessy Street, Vancouver, British Columbia V6P 6E5

10 9 8 7 6 5 4 3 2 1

Chronicle Books LLC
85 Second Street, San Francisco, California 94105

www.chroniclekids.com